D0844702

Jack the Puppy

**For a free color catalog describing Gareth Stevens' list
of high-quality children's books call 1 (800) 433-0942**

Library of Congress Cataloging-in-Publication Data

Burton, Jane.
     Jack the puppy / by Jane Burton. — North American ed.
       p. cm. — (Baby animals growing up)
    Includes index.
    Summary: Text and photographs present Jack the puppy's first year
of life as he plays with his nine brothers and sisters and grows larger.
    ISBN 0-8368-0209-8
    1. Puppies—Juvenile literature. 2. Dogs—Development—Juvenile
literature. [1. Dogs. 2. Animals—Infancy.] I. Title.II. Series: Burton, Jane.
Baby animals growing up.
SF426.5.B87   1989
636.7'07—dc20   89-11422

This North American edition first published in 1989 by

Gareth Stevens Children's Books
7317 W. Green Tree Road
Milwaukee, Wisconsin 53223, USA

Format © 1989 by Gareth Stevens, Inc. Supplementary text © 1989 by
Gareth Stevens, Inc. Original text and photographs © 1988 by Jane Burton.
First published in Great Britain in 1988 by Macdonald & Co. Ltd.

Editors: Patricia Lantier and Rhoda Irene Sherwood
Cover design: Kate Kriege

Printed in the United States of America

1 2 3 4 5 6 7 8 9 95 94 93 92 91 90 89

**Baby
Animals
Growing
Up!**

Jack the Puppy

JANE BURTON

Gareth Stevens Children's Books
MILWAUKEE

Jack is Honey's tenth puppy. As soon as he was born, Honey cleaned and dried him with her tongue. For many minutes Jack lay all limp, not breathing or moving. Then he gave a gasp and his legs began to twitch. Soon he was scrambling among his brothers and sisters to find a spot where he could feed.

Puppies are born with their eyes and ears
closed so they cannot see or hear anything.
They find their way by smell and feel. When
Jack feeds, he kneads Honey's milkbags with
his paws to make the milk flow.

Eleven days old

The puppies can crawl along on their tummies but cannot walk yet. They crawl all over each other and squirm and wriggle when Honey tries to wash them. She holds Jack with her paw to keep him still while she licks.

Jack can nearly climb over the side of the box. But his eyes are just opening, so if he topples right out, he might get lost or cold. Luckily, he decides to slide backward the way he came.

Eighteen days old

Grandmother Tess is baby-sitting in the box with some of her eleven "grandpuppies" while Honey is out for a walk.

Tess can keep the puppies warm and clean and guard them from danger. She even lets them try to feed, but she can only make a little milk for them.

Honey has been away for a long time, and Jack and his brothers and sisters are getting hungry. Now that their eyes are open, they watch for their mother to come back.

The puppies can easily climb out of the box. They scamper about all over the floor and play fighting games. Fan nips Jack while Digger pounces on Fan. Their milk teeth are very sharp, but too tiny to hurt each other.

Four weeks old

On a warm day the puppies toddle outside and explore the yard. They soon find a puddle. Jack is not sure he likes getting his paws wet.

Honey is a very patient mother. She puts up with Jack's chewing her ear when she is trying to sleep.

Six weeks old

The puppies are finally able to eat solid food. They each have their own bowl, but it is not long before they are swapping bowls and trying to gobble up someone else's dinner.

Poor Jack stumbles into the pond! How was
he to know floating weed was not solid ground?
He knows how to swim by instinct, so he puppy-
paddles to the edge and is helped out and licked
dry. Jack goes back to lick Gem and Allie, who
have also fallen in.

Ten weeks old

The puppies find a large toad in their yard. Each puppy picks it up, but quickly spits it out again. It tastes very nasty, and makes them froth at the mouth and shake their heads. But they are fascinated by it and want to play with it. Jack watches intently as it hops along, and Emma invites it to play with her. But they dare not touch it again.

Four months old

In spite of falling into the pond, the puppies are not afraid of water. On hot days Jack and Emma jump into the pond on purpose and pick the water lilies.

At the end of summer, Jack and Lady go berrying among the bushes. They reach up to pick the low fruit very delicately, being careful not to spike their muzzles on the prickles.

Five months old

The puppies are large and boisterous; their games are rough and noisy. Jack is the most boisterous and noisy of them all. He is losing his baby teeth. He gnaws a tough leather toy to help his big teeth come through.

When Jack bites Lady, even in play, he can hurt her, although he may not mean to. Sometimes Honey joins in their romp. The way they all bite and snarl and wrestle, it sometimes looks and sounds as if they are having a real dogfight. But they are playing.

The blue ball is Jack's favorite toy. He chases after it, tosses it in the air, and chews it. He runs past the other dogs with it, daring them to chase him.

Six months old

One bright, cold winter morning, the pups go down to the beach. They run through the shallow ponds and in and out to the sea until their coats are soaking wet.

Dogs have a special way of drying themselves.
They shake themselves all over. The shake
starts with the head, moves down the entire
body, and ends with the tail. The water sprays
out all around, leaving the dog nearly dry again.

Seven months old

At first Jack, Lady, and Fan were puzzled by the snow. Then they went wild, pouncing and rolling in it and chasing each other. They ran and ran in the big field because they were so excited by the snow.

21

Eight months old

Jack wants whatever Lady finds to play with. When he sees her with the stuffed toy, he tries to grab it. Lady holds on tight, so they have a great tussle — sometimes running along together with it, sometimes tugging in opposite directions. When Jack cannot get the toy by tugging, he tries rolling to twist it out of Lady's mouth.

Sometimes Lady gets tired and Jack gets the toy. But it is all a game. Jack's playful face tells Lady that he wants her to pounce on him and try to take the toy back again.

23

Twelve months old

Jack now has seven new baby brothers and sisters. Honey would not let him near the box when the new puppies were tiny. But now that they are eight weeks old and able to waddle outdoors, Jack is allowed to play with them.

Little Rosie puts her muzzle right inside Jack's mouth, hoping he will share his dinner with her. If he feels generous or kind, he will bring up a neat little helping of food for Rosie to eat. This is the way dogs feed solid food to puppies. Dogs can carry a lot more in their stomachs than they can in their mouths. Jack is always eating, so his stomach probably holds more than enough food for himself — and for the pups as well! Rosie gets some, and the others will want some too.

It is Jack's first birthday; he is one year old today. The yard where he used to romp with his ten brothers and sisters is alive with little puppies again. Jack is surprisingly gentle with these babies. One day he may have puppies of his own to guard and play with.

Fun Facts About Puppies (and Dogs)

1. Puppies have 32 temporary teeth, which they begin to lose when they are about five months old. Adult dogs have 42 teeth.

2. A whelp is an unweaned puppy — that is, one that still feeds on its mother's milk. The term also means to give birth to puppies.

3. Whelping normally takes anywhere from 45 minutes to 2 hours for a litter of seven puppies.

4. At least 12,000 years ago, dogs became the first animals to be tamed.

5. A shar-pei puppy's skin is so loose that it appears to be too large for the dog's body.

6. The basenji, which originated in Africa, is the only dog that cannot bark.

7. By the age of four weeks, a puppy can produce a dog's full range of vocal sounds — barks, growls, howls, whines, and yelps. Some of these sounds have different meanings in different situations.

8. Puppies love to chew on bones. But the only kind of bone that is safe is the shinbone from a cow. Other bones splinter and can become caught in a dog's throat.

9. Here is how to carry a puppy so it feels safe and comfortable: Hold your arms like a cradle. One arm fits under the puppy's chest in front of its legs. The other arm fits under its rear end behind its legs.

10. Since puppies and dogs don't like to take medicine when they are sick, experts suggest hiding pills inside meatballs of liverwurst or canned dog meat.

For More Information About Animal Life

Listed below are some books, magazines, and videocassettes that contain interesting information about dogs. See if they are in your local library or bookstore or if someone there can order them for you.

Books
Caring for Your Dog. McPherson (Troll)
Clever and Courageous Dogs. Finlay and Hancock (David & Charles)
A Dog's Body. Cole (Morrow)
Dog and Puppies. Hill; Goaman, editor (EDC)
Five True Dog Stories. Davidson (Scholastic)
I Want A Dog. Khalsa (Crown)
The Last Puppy. Asch (Prentice-Hall)
The Life of a Dog. Feder (Childrens Press)
My First Puppy. Hausherr (Macmillan)
Playful Pups. Wolf, editor (Antioch)
Puppies. Rinard (National Geographic)
A Puppy Is Born.   Fischer-Nagel and Fisher-Nagel (Putnam)

Magazines
Chickadee
Young Naturalist Foundation
P.O. Box 11314
Des Moines, IA 50340

Owl
Young Naturalist Foundation
P.O. Box 11314
Des Moines, IA 50340

National Geographic World
National Geographic Society
P.O. Box 2330
Washington, DC 20013-9865

Ranger Rick
National Wildlife Federation
8925 Leesburg Pike
Vienna, VA 22184-0001

Videocassettes
The Puppy's Amazing Rescue. Coronet Instructional Films, 1980.
The Puppy's Great Adventure. Coronet Instructional Films, 1979.

Things to Do

1. If you have your own puppy or dog, draw and color a picture of it. Then in a short paragraph describe how your pet is important to you and your family. Be sure to include your dog's name on the picture.

If you don't happen to own a puppy or dog, do the same exercise by drawing a picture of the puppy you would like to have. Look for pictures of dogs in encyclopedias or library books so you can see all the different kinds there are.

2. Why are dogs such good pets? Make a list of the good qualities dogs have, and then explain why someone might choose to own a dog instead of some other type of pet.

3. What are some of the games you might play with your dog? Name the games and explain them briefly to a friend or family member.

4. Are all dogs good pets for everyone? Find out about those kinds of dogs that might not be good family pets and explain why. What dogs would be good pets if you lived in a city apartment? Which ones are better in rural areas?

5. Try to arrange a trip with some friends and a parent to a nearby pet shop. Spend extra time looking at the puppies, and try to learn what "type" of dog each one is. If there is time, see if you and your friends can agree on a possible name for each dog, a name that would seem to fit its personality.

6. Many local governments have had to pass laws about dogs so that the cities remain safe and clean. Try to find out what restrictions there are on owning dogs in your area. Must dogs be kept on leashes? Are people required to carry scoops to clean up dog feces when they walk their dogs?

Things to Talk About

1. As soon as Jack and his brothers and sisters can see, they watch for their mother's return when she leaves for a while. When members of your family leave, do you sometimes watch at the window, waiting for them to come home? Why do you think this is so?

2. Jack accidentally falls into a pond, but he is in no real danger because he knows how to swim instinctively. What does this mean? Do humans know how to swim instinctively?

3. When Jack and his brothers and sisters play, it is often noisy and rough. Is this how you play with your own brothers and sisters? Are there other ways to play besides being loud? Give some examples.

4. Dogs dry themselves by shaking their coats until they are nearly water-free. How do people dry themselves after they get wet? Can you name more than one way?

5. Jack very soon has new brothers and sisters. He is curious about them, but his mother won't let him come near the babies yet. Why is this so? Are you curious about new babies? Are you sometimes allowed to get a close look at a newborn baby or to hold it?

6. As his new brothers and sisters get a little older, Jack shares his food with them and treats them gently. What are some of the nice things you can do for a new baby?

7. Jack is one year old at the end of this book. Do you think he will have a birthday party? Why are birthday parties important to children?

8. When Jack gets new brothers and sisters, he is no longer one of the babies. His actions change; because he is an "older" brother, he begins to act older. How is this like the life of a human child?

Glossary of New Words

boisterous: very noisy and lively

gnaw: to chew on or bite with the teeth

gobble: to eat quickly and greedily

knead: to massage; to press, rub, or squeeze

muzzle: the front part of the head of an animal, which includes the mouth, nose, and jaws

paw: the hand or foot of a four-footed animal

pounce: to jump on or spring at something or someone

prickles: small, sharp thorns that grow on the outer layers of some plants

romp: to play in a very lively manner

scamper: to run around or play quickly or hurriedly

snarl: to growl fiercely, often baring the teeth

toddle: to walk with small, uncertain steps, like a baby

tug: to pull at with great strength or force

tussle: to wrestle or scuffle; to fight

whelping box: a special place set aside for mother animals to have their babies

Index